Usborne Phonics Readers
Fat cat on a mat

Phil Roxbee Cox
Illustrated by Stephen Cartwright
Edited by Jenny Tyler

Language consultant: Marlynne Grant
BSc, CertEd, MEdPsych, PhD, AFBPs, CPsychol

There is a little yellow duck to find on every page.

First published in 2006 by Usborne Publishing Ltd., Usborne House, 83-85 Saffron Hill, London EC1N 8RT, England. www.usborne.com
Copyright © 2006, 1999 Usborne Publishing Ltd.

Fat Cat sees a bee.

BUZZ

Fat Cat flees up a tree.
"I don't like bees!" yelps Fat Cat.

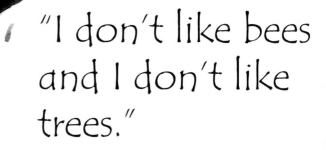

"I don't like bees and I don't like trees."

"I don't like bees *or* trees."

"Are you stuck?"
shouts Big Pig.

"Bad luck!" shouts Big Pig.

Fat Cat
groans.

"I am stuck.
It *is* bad luck,"
she moans.

The tree bends...

7

The nest drops,
with a plop, on
top of Big Pig.

"Like my new hat, Fat Cat?"

"Good catch!"
yelps Fat Cat.

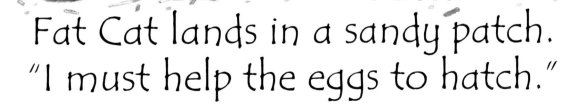

Fat Cat lands in a sandy patch.
"I must help the eggs to hatch."

Next day,

Fat Cat will
not play.

"Play with me!" says Big Pig.

"Not today," says Fat Cat on her mat.

"Bake a cake with me,"
says Jake Snake.

"Not today," says Fat Cat on her mat.

"Let's run in the sun for fun," says Ted.

"Not today," says Fat Cat on her mat.

"You are lazy," says Big Pig.
"You are crazy," says Jake Snake.

"You are no fun," says Ted.

"Shh!" says
Fat Cat.

"Stay away,"
says Fat Cat.

Clever Fat Cat!